Snappy Crocodile Tale

By Niki Foreman

Penguin Random House

LONDON, NEW YORK, MUNICH,
MELBOURNE, AND DELHI

DK LONDON
Series Editor Deborah Lock
Editorial Assistant Katy Lennon
US Senior Editor Shannon Beatty
Senior Art Editor Ann Cannings
Producer, Pre-production Francesca Wardell

Reading Consultant Linda Gambrell, Ph.D.

DK DELHI
Editor Pomona Zaheer
Art Editor Yamini Panwar
DTP Designers Anita Yadav,
Sachin Gupta, Nityanand Kumar
Picture Researcher Surya Sarangi
Managing Editor Soma B. Chowdhury
Managing Art Editor Ahlawat Gunjan

First American Edition, 2015
Published in the United States by DK Publishing
345 Hudson Street, New York, New York 10014

14 15 16 17 10 9 8 7 6 5 4 3 2 1
001—273238—January/2015

Published in Great Britain by Dorling Kindersley Limited.

A catalog record for this book is availablefrom the Library of Congress.
ISBN: 978-1-4654-2837-0 (Paperback)
ISBN: 978-1-4654-2835-6 (Hardback)

DK books are available at special discounts when purchased in bulk for sales promotions,
premiums, fund-raising, or educational use. For details, contact:
DK Publishing Special Markets
345 Hudson Street, New York, New York 10014
SpecialSales@dk.com

Printed and bound in China by South China Printing Company.

The publisher would like to thank the following for their kind permission
to reproduce their photographs:
(Key: a-above; b-below/bottom; c-center; f-far; l-left; r-right; t-top)
1 Getty Images: Ian Waldie/Getty Images News. **4 Corbis**: Nature Connect (t). **5 Alamy Images**: Blickwinkel/Schmidbauer (b).
6 Dreamstime.com: Tjkphotography (b). **9 Getty Images**: Reinhard Dirscherl/Visuals Unlimited, Inc. **11 Corbis**: David
Watts/Visuals Unlimited. **12 Dreamstime.com**: Hotshotsworldwide (br); Stanko Mravljak (cl). **12–13 Corbis**: Buddy Mays
(Background); **Dreamstime.com**: Yael Weiss (Magnifying glass). **13 Corbis**: Gavriel Jecan (tl); Buddy Mays (cr);
Dreamstime.com: Germanshooter (bl). **14 Corbis**: Luigi Vaccarella/SOPA. **15 Corbis**: Jeffrey L. Rotman. **16–17 Getty
Images**: Richard I'Anson/Lonely Planet Images. **18 Corbis**: 2/Natphotos/Ocean. **21 Getty Images**: Auscape/Contributor/
Universal Images Group. **22 Fotolia**: Peter Wey (b). **22–23 Corbis**: Buddy Mays (Background); **Dreamstime.com**: Alenapohu
(Wooden frames). **23 Dreamstime.com**: Siloto (t); **Getty Images**: Tier Und Naturfotografie J und C Sohns/Photographer's
Choice (c). **24–25 Corbis**: Buddy Mays (Background). **26 Getty Images**: Ted Mead/Photolibrary. **27 Getty Images**: Dea/
C.dani/I.jeske/Contributor/De Agostini (b). **28–29 Getty Images**: Peter Walton Photography/Photolibrary. **31 Getty Images**:
Keren Su/China Span. **32–33 Getty Images**: Victoria Stone & Mark Deeble/Oxford Scientific. **34 Dorling Kindersley**:
Jerry Young (cr); **Getty Images**: Nature, underwater and art photos. www.Narchuk.com/Moment Open (cla). **35 Dorling
Kindersley**: Jerry Young (cl); National Birds of Prey Centre, Gloucestershire (tl); Philip Dowell (cr). **36 Alamy Images**:
Daniel Jones and Laura Johnson. **37 Alamy Images**: Linda Weissenberger. **38 Getty Images**: Jonathan and Angela Scott/
The Image Bank. **40–41 Corbis**: Radius Images. **42–43 Corbis**: Michael Pitts/Nature Picture Library. **44–45 Corbis**: Buddy
Mays (Background). **45 Dreamstime.com**: Venusangel (br). **46 Dreamstime.com**: Ashley Whitworth. **47 Getty Images**:
Jason Edwards/National Geographic. **48–49 Dreamstime.com**: Timothy Lubcke. **50–51 Dreamstime.com**: Ralph Lohse.
52–53 Corbis: W. Perry Conway. **54–55 Corbis**: Buddy Mays (Background); **Dreamstime.com**: Deboracilli (c, Frames at
the corners). **55 Corbis**: PoodlesRock/GraphicaArtis (cr); Dreamstime.com: DeboracaArtis (br). **56–57 Corbis**: Buddy Mays
(Background). **58–59 Corbis**: Buddy Mays (Background). **58 Fotolia**: Vadim Yerofeyev (c/Road sign)
Jacket images: Front: Dreamstime.com: Hel080808; **Back: Dreamstime.com**: Ralph Lohse (tl), Tjkphotography (cra);
Spine: Dreamstime.com: Hotshotsworldwide (b)

All other images © Dorling Kindersley
For further information see: www.dkimages.com

Discover more at
www.dk.com

Contents

Chapter 1
Born to be Wild

The big red sun cast its rays over the snaking Alligator River of Kakadu National Park, Australia. A lone log drifted downstream, carried along by the tumbling water—two beady eyes sitting on top of the log.

With a sudden splash, the log turned and slowly swam back upstream, but it wasn't a log; it was a crocodile! Its movements rippled through the water, hitting a mound of branches and mud on the sandy bank—a crocodile nest. Nestled in the mud were 57 large, leathery eggs. One tipped over and a muffled chirping broke out.

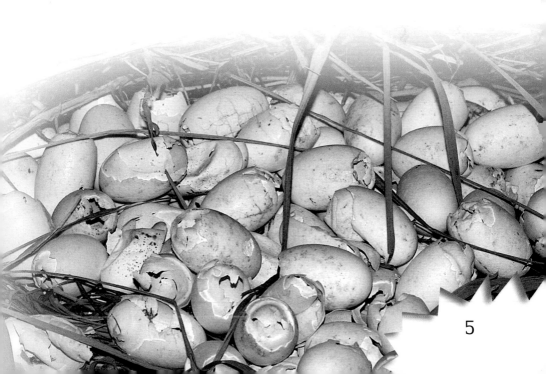

"Chirp, chirp! What's going on out there?" wondered Christopher Crocodile inside his tipped-over egg. Using the small egg tooth on his upper snout, he chip, chip, chipped at the eggshell. A small crack appeared. Chris Croc wriggled and writhed through the crack, and landed head-first in the muddy nest.

A giant jaw of teeth appeared out of nowhere!

It picked up an egg and rolled it around its huge mouth. CRACK! Another baby crocodile appeared.

"Thanks, Mom!" it chirped. The mother crocodile lowered the baby into the nest.

A gang of other newly hatched baby crocodiles had crept up behind Chris Croc. They lunged forward. Chris Croc turned on his tail, but a wall of mud-caked twigs was in his way! Floating above the wall, his mother's big eyes stared right at him. They were attached to her giant jaw of teeth. Her long snout rested on the nest wall and snapped open. The gang scrambled inside.

"Hi, Mom!" squeaked Chris Croc as he followed.

"Watch out for my teeth!" the mother crocodile said.
Chris Croc looked up as razor-sharp gnashers came down on them...

Suddenly her mouth opened again and water flooded in.
Chris Croc and the others rushed into the river's cool, murky water.

"Stick to the shallows!" the mother crocodile warned.

But Chris Croc was eager to explore everywhere! He held his breath and dived down beneath the river surface.

Special flaps of see-through skin shot across his eyes, helping him to see under the water. He spied a plump shrimp on the river bed.

"Snack time!" he thought with a grin, but a cloud of mud swept up from the river bed. The tasty-looking shrimp was gone!

Something fast and furry swam out of the muddy water. Chris Croc followed. The strange-looking creature had a flat, duckbill snout at the front and a beaver's tail at the back. Its furry cheek bulged with something. Chris Croc could guess what that was!

"That's my shrimp!" he shouted.

The duckbill platypus munched on the small shrimp. Then in a flash of fur and a burst of bubbles, it was gone.

The setting sun dipped below the horizon. Chris Croc swam back to his mother in the shallows, wondering what other curious creatures were around.

Crocodiles Close-up

Saltwater crocodiles like Chris Croc are the largest living reptiles and more aggressive than their smaller freshwater cousins. Here are some of the features that help them thrive in the wild.

◀ Eyes

Crocodiles' pupils get bigger to let in more light, making it easier for crocodiles to see in the dark.

Teeth

Crocodiles lose many teeth throughout their lives. However, they are always able to grow brand-new ones in the same place.

◀Eyes and nostrils

Crocodiles have eyes and nostrils on top of their heads so that they can hide under water and still be able to see and breathe.

Scales or scutes▶

Crocodile scales are strengthened with bone, which makes the crocs' skin tough, protecting them like armor.

◀Mouths

When crocodiles are too hot, they leave their mouths open in order to let out heat.

Chapter 2
Attack

The raucous squawk of
a cockatoo echoed through the
valley. The sun peeped over the
horizon, casting dappled spots of
light through the trees. A group
of young crocodiles watched
a flickering spot of sunlight.

Their pale yellow bodies were almost camouflaged in the sunny glare—except for the black spots on their backs. Chris Croc bounded out of the river shallows. His four strong legs carried him faster and faster. He gained pace across the sandy ground and pounced on the spot of light. He sneaked a look under his foot, but the ground started shaking...

The crocodiles rushed back to the river as two large animals bounced to its edge.

"Phew!" Chris Croc thought. "They're after a drink, not a crocodile! But what are they?"

Chris Croc edged closer for a better look when one of them started thumping the ground with its long, strong back legs. It had noticed Chris Croc and didn't look happy to see him.

"Don't come any closer with those teeth!" it warned. "I have a killer kick, and I'm not afraid to use it!"

The thumper jumper watched Chris Croc, and Chris Croc stared right back.

"Hello," Chris Croc said. "I'm sorry to scare you, but what are you?"

"We're wallabies, of course!" exclaimed the thumper, who became more jumpy as the rest of the crocodiles came closer.

The two wallabies did a bouncy dance around the bank, making the crocodiles laugh.

But Chris Croc felt like they were being watched. He scanned the trees. His gaze locked on a pair of eyes.

"But trees don't have eyes, do they?" he thought.

In the blink of an eye, a long goanna had run down the tree and into the group of crocodiles. Bands of black with spots of white marked its scaly body. It gobbled up a young crocodile and licked its lips with a lash of its forked tongue. The sharp claws on its strong foot pinned down another young crocodile.

The spooked wallabies fled and the rest of the crocodiles swam to safety. Chris Croc watched. He decided to grow healthy and strong, so that nothing would consider eating him as a snack— ever again.

Family Differences

Crocodiles, alligators, caimans, and gharials all belong to a group of animals known as crocodilians. Crocodilians have many similar features and can live both in and out of water. But how can we tell them all apart?

Crocodile

Crocodiles have teeth that stick out over their jaws.

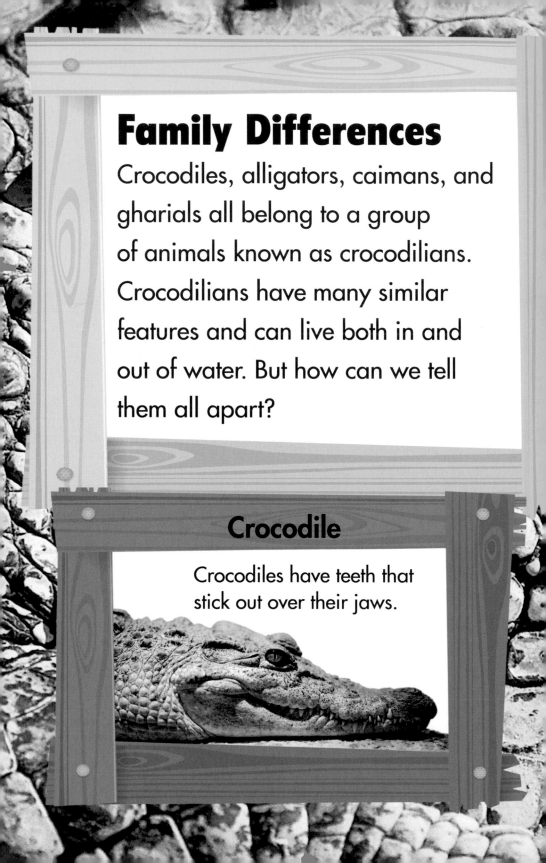

Gharial

Gharials have long, thin snouts that they use to snap up birds and fish to eat.

Alligator

Alligators have short, wide snouts to catch large prey.

Caiman

Caimans are the smallest members of the family and often reach only 6.5 ft (2 m) in length.

Where in the World?

Crocodilians live all over the world.
This map shows the areas where
we can expect to find them.

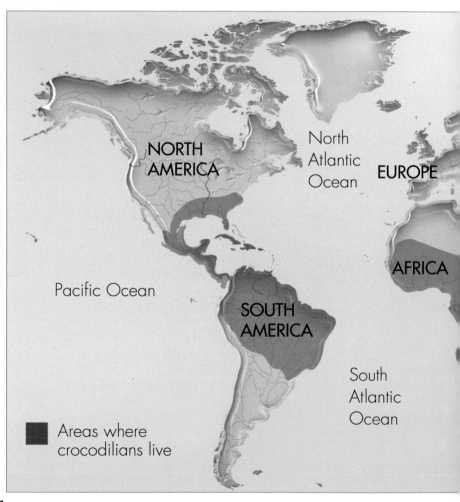

NORTH
AMERICA

North
Atlantic
Ocean

EUROPE

AFRICA

Pacific Ocean

SOUTH
AMERICA

South
Atlantic
Ocean

Areas where
crocodilians live

Crocodiles
Africa, North and South America, Southeast Asia, Australia

Caimans
Central and South America

Alligators
USA and China

Gharials
South Asia

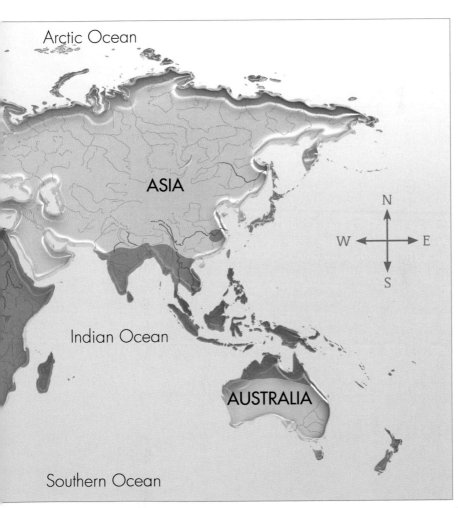

Arctic Ocean

ASIA

N
W ← → E
S

Indian Ocean

AUSTRALIA

Southern Ocean

Chapter 3
The Big Eat

The fiery sun beat down on
the dry, bristly bush and towering
termite mounds. A swarm of
termites scurried from their
nest into the wooded wetlands.
Lying there in the scrub, a newly
matured saltwater crocodile

basked in the sun. His scaly body had darkened to a dirty gray, and bony scutes armed his back and tail. Chris Croc stretched his heavy jaw wide open. His soft pants expelled hot air, and his 68 spikelike teeth flashed in the sun. His nostrils flared as he caught a smell.

A crackling sound caught Chris Croc's attention. A smoky taste filled his mouth as a thick fog of smoke spiraled into the air.

BUSHFIRE!

A high-pitched screech from a lorikeet jerked Chris Croc into action. He could feel the fire's burning heat as it ate everything in its path. Chris Croc crawled across the ground to the river, where his powerful tail propelled him away from the heat and into the deep, cool water. Splashes all around gave away other animals trying to escape the fire. Chris Croc smiled to himself. Dinner is served!

Chris Croc slowly swam closer to the sandy riverbank. Wallabies splashed, snakes slithered, and dingoes ducked their heads in the shallows. Then came the real prize… a herd of water buffalo ran along the riverbank. A young calf ventured into the water, looking to escape from the heat. Chris Croc slowly but surely floated closer to it. With just his eyes and nostrils above the surface so he could see and breathe, Chris Croc moved into position and waited…

SPLASH!

Chris Croc burst out of the water. His jaws slammed shut around the calf's throat, tightening and crushing it. He dragged it into deeper water and plunged beneath the surface where he rolled it in an underwater dance.

When all signs of life had
left his catch, Chris Croc swam
to the surface. He thrashed his
head to rip off chunks of meat
as it started to pour with rain.
Chris Croc's eyes twinkled,
reflecting the dying bushfire.

Friend or Foe?

Follow the green lines to find out what some crocodiles like to eat, and follow the red lines to discover some animals that eat crocodiles—especially baby ones!

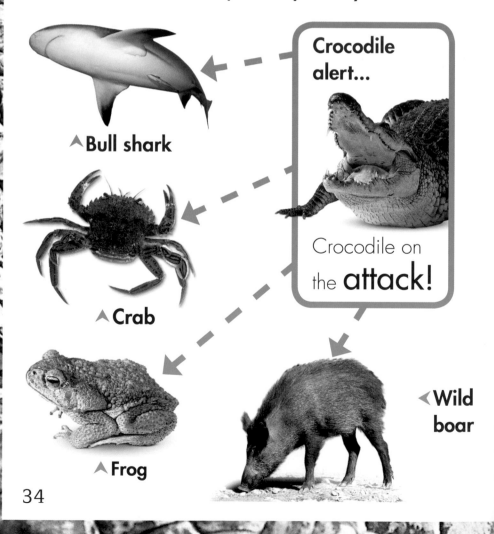

▲ Bull shark

Crocodile alert...

Crocodile on the **attack!**

▲ Crab

◄ Wild boar

▲ Frog

35

Chapter 4
Strange Encounter

Chris Croc was getting too big for his britches. His hunting skills hadn't gone unnoticed by other, bigger male crocodiles in the river. One large crocodile in particular did not like Chris Croc being in his watery territory.

Unaware of the powerful crocodile seeking him out, Chris Croc lazed in the shallows. All was still around him—too still… Then the monstrous male launched a surprise attack. Its head smashed down on Chris Croc's body.

"Owwww!" cried Chris Croc. He swung his head to face his attacker, but suffered another head-smash, this time on his upper jaw.

Chris Croc was beaten. He powered a getaway through the water and headed downstream, nursing his sore bruises.

After a long morning swimming downstream, Chris Croc found himself in rougher water that tasted salty. He must be close to the ocean! Golden cliffs of sandstone lined the waterway. Waves lapped at his body, and the midday sun beat down on his scaly skin.

Chris Croc found a shaded bank to rest on. He looked around him at the stark cliffs. White lines on a nearby rockface painted a picture that looked just like him. The paintings continued along the rocky outcrop. Intrigued, Chris Croc followed them into the bristly bushland. He came to a clearing, but something bit him on the nose!

"Ouch!"

An electric fence stretched up to the treetops, and inside the fence were other crocodiles!

"What are they all doing in there?" Chris Croc wondered, as a twig cracked just behind him…

Crocodile Farm

Two thin, weak animals with small heads on their long, lean bodies stood behind Chris Croc on their hind legs, pointing a long stick at him. Chris Croc ran, and the stick went BANG!

"Get him!" one of them shouted. "He's a big 'un. He needs to go in the croc farm!"

Chris Croc crashed through the undergrowth and plunged into the river. He held his breath and swam as fast and as far as he could under water. He didn't know what a crocodile farm was, but he did know that he didn't like those biting fences and banging sticks.

Save the Crocs Debate

This motion proposes that crocodiles should not be hunted.

For

Many types of crocodile have been in danger of dying out in recent years. We need crocodiles to stay alive because they play a big part in keeping wetlands working as a healthy habitat. They play their part in the food chain and many other animals rely on them. Crocodiles are among some of the oldest types of animals alive on Earth today. It would be a great loss if such an ancient animal died out completely because of the actions of humans.

44

Against

Crocodiles are a nuisance and
a threat to the human race.
Crocodiles are pests, and in many
countries, they eat cattle and attack
humans. Hunting crocodiles helps
to get rid of this threat and provides
people with many chances to sell
them for money. Crocodile skin
clothes and shoes are very popular
with people and can be sold for
high prices. Many countries also eat
crocodile meat, so hunting them
provides an extra food resource.

Chapter 5
A New Guy in Town

The sun peeped over the sandstone cliffs. Chris Croc skulked in the shade in the brackish water. At 30 years old, he was big and strong and at the top of the food chain.

Just downstream, another large, male crocodile slunk into the water. Chris Croc eyed the unwelcome guest. He arched his long, strong tail, heaved his head high, and smashed it down into the water. The warning boom bounced off the sandstone surroundings, scaring the intruder away and out of Chris Croc's territory.

Pleased with his victory, Chris Croc slipped into the sun-kissed water, but something large was swimming below him.

"That pesky crocodile's back again!" Chris Croc thought to himself.

But it didn't look or swim like a crocodile...

For a start, it had a funny fin
on its back, and that fin was
slicing through the water, heading
straight for him.

It was a bull shark!

Chris Croc sank under the water
to meet the bullish predator head-on.
A wide jaw of knifelike teeth came
at him through the water.

The bull shark landed a painful bite on Chris Croc's tough torso, but Chris Croc swung around and bit the bull shark right back. The two carnivores were strong challengers and neither of them wanted to lose the fight.

They thrashed around in the water trying their best to scare the other away. Finally, Chris Croc landed the winning blow. The bull shark realized it was defeated and turned on its tail, swimming away as fast as it could.

Chris Croc, king of his territory, cruised down the river enjoying the warm afternoon sun. He saw the mother of his babies looking after their hatchlings. The tiny crocs chirped happily as they hopped into their mother's mouth, ready for their first swim in the river.

Chris Croc swam on to
his favorite basking spot
to catch the last of the sun's
rays. At the edge of the river,
he relaxed, but with one eye
open—ready and waiting for
any predator who would dare
to challenge him next!

The Creation of Ginga

This story is set in the Dreamtime.
The Dreamtime is when aboriginal people of
Australia believe that the world was created.

ঔ৶ ঔ৶ ঔ৶ ঔ৶ ঔ৶

At the beginning of time, before the world was created, there was a man who lived near a river. One day, he was sleeping next to a fire to keep warm. In his sleep, he rolled too close to the flames. His back caught fire, and the man jumped up and ran to the river. He jumped into the river to put out the flames. The fire and water formed blisters on his back, which turned him into a giant crocodile.

The crocodile was named Ginga. Ginga lived on the land and in the water and crawled along the ground to travel between his two habitats. Ginga used his wide snout to push through the earth and rocks and create paths between the dry land and the water. Over time, the paths became deeper and deeper, and after many years, large mountains began to form around the river.

Once Ginga had finished sculpting the landscape, he knew that his job was done and he turned himself to stone. His jagged back can still be seen today in the rocky hills of Kakadu National Park.

Dotty Rock Painting

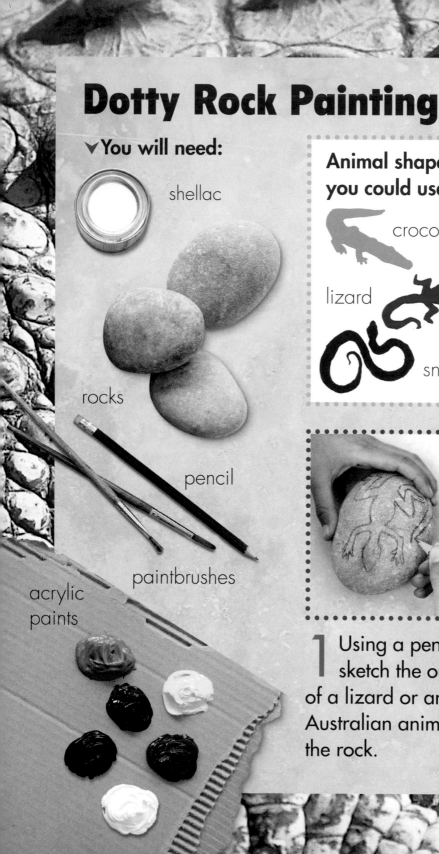

▼You will need:

shellac

rocks

pencil

paintbrushes

acrylic paints

Animal shapes you could use:

crocodile

lizard

snake

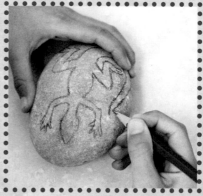

1 Using a pencil, sketch the outline of a lizard or another Australian animal on the rock.

2 Use orange paint for the background around the shape. Allow this to dry, and then paint the animal.

3 Make a line of white dots all around the shape. Then fill in the background with other colored dots.

Paint on eyes.

4 Next make lines of yellow dots inside the animal shape. Add a red dot inside each yellow dot to finish the pattern.

Add shellac for a shiny finish.

Crocodile Safety
Kakadu Campgrounds

DANGER

✔ **Do** look out for crocodile signs. These warn you that crocodiles may be around.

✘ **Don't** swim in the water. This is where crocodiles might be hiding!

✔ **Do** take all your garbage with you when you leave the park. Crocodiles may enter the area because of the smell.

✘ **Don't** set up your tent near the water's edge. Crocodiles might sneak up on you when you are asleep!

✘ **Don't** get too close to crocodiles. They are not friendly animals!

Crocodile Tale Quiz

1. Where are crocodiles' eyes and nostrils found on their heads?

2. How can you tell the difference between a crocodile and an alligator?

3. Where in the world can you expect to find alligators?

4. How do hatchlings get from their nest to the water?

5. What made all the animals run toward the water in Chapter 3?

Answers on page 61.

Glossary

aboriginal people
people who lived
in the land from
the earliest time

adaptation
when an animal's
body changes over
generations, helping it
to survive in its habitat

bask
relax in the sun and
enjoy its warmth

camouflage
markings on the skin
that match an animal's
surroundings, helping
it to hide

habitat
place where an
animal naturally lives

nocturnal
when an animal stays
awake at night but
sleeps during the day

scutes
hard bony plates
on the scaly skin
of some reptiles

territory
area of land controlled
by a certain person,
animal, or group

Index

Answers to the Crocodile Tale Quiz:
1. On top of their heads; **2.** Crocodiles have long, narrow snouts with teeth that stick out over their jaws; **3.** USA and China; **4.** In their mother's mouth; **5.** A bushfire.

Guide for Parents

DK Readers is a four-level interactive reading adventure series for children, developing the habit of reading widely for both pleasure and information. These books have an exciting main narrative interspersed with a range of reading genres to suit your child's reading ability, as required by the Common Core State Standards. Each book is designed to develop your child's reading skills, fluency, grammar awareness, and comprehension in order to build confidence and engagement when reading.

Ready for a *Reading Alone* book

YOUR CHILD SHOULD

- be able to read most words without needing to stop and break them down into sound parts.

- read smoothly, in phrases and with expression. By this level, your child will be mostly reading silently.

- self-correct when some word or sentence doesn't sound right.

A VALUABLE AND SHARED READING EXPERIENCE

For some children, text reading, particularly non-fiction, requires much effort, but adult participation can make this both fun and easier. So here are a few tips on how to use this book with your child.

TIP 1 Check out the contents together before your child begins:

- invite your child to check the blurb, contents page, and layout of the book and comment on it.

- ask your child to make predictions about the story.

- talk about the information your child might want to find out.

TIP 2 Encourage fluent and flexible reading:

- support your child to read in fluent, expressive phrases, making full use of punctuation and thinking about the meaning.

- encourage your child to slow down and check information where appropriate.

TIP 3 Indicators that your child is reading for meaning:

- your child will be responding to the text if he/she is self-correcting and varying his/her voice
- your child will want to talk about what he/she is reading or is eager to turn the page to find out what will happen next.

TIP 4 Share and discuss:

- encourage your child to recall specific details after each chapter.
- provide opportunities for your child to pick out interesting words and discuss what they mean.
- discuss how the author captures the reader's interest, or how effective the non-fiction layouts are.
- ask questions about the text. These help to develop comprehension skills and awareness of the language used.

A FEW ADDITIONAL TIPS

- Read to your child regularly to demonstrate fluency, phrasing, and expression; to find out or check information; and for sharing enjoyment.
- Encourage your child to reread favorite texts to increase reading confidence and fluency.
- Check that your child is reading a range of different types of material, such as poems, jokes, and following instructions.

Series consultant, **Dr. Linda Gambrell**, Distinguished Professor of Education at Clemson University, has served as President of the National Reading Conference, the College Reading Association, and the International Reading Association. She is also reading consultant for the **DK Adventures**.

Have you read these other great books from DK?

Meet the sharks who live on the reef or come passing through.

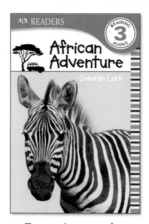

Experience the thrill of seeing wild animals on an African safari.

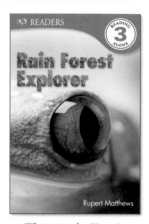

Through Zoe's blog, discover the mysteries of the Amazon.

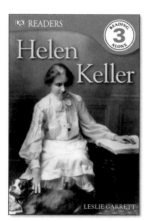

Read about the remarkable story of the deaf-blind girl who achieved great things.

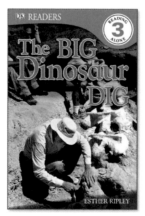

Josh and his team dig up dinosaur bones in a race against time.

This is the incredible true story of the "unsinkable" ship that sank.